Here, There And Everywhere

My journey from lost to found

Harini Mahadevan

Made with ❤ on the BookLeaf Publishing Platform
www.bookleafpub.in
www.bookleafpub.com

Dedication

To Ma, the reason I write.

To Pa, the reason I dream.

To Akshay, the reason I healed.

Preface

I believe poetry offers a sneak peek into a writer's mind in the most beautiful and profound of ways. I started writing poems at the age of 12 — before I even fully understood what poetry meant. Words simply began to form in my mind and writing them down was a way to let them go, to make sense of the noise.

Seventeen years later, here we are.

This book is a collection of moments — curated experiences from my journey through childhood, adolescence, and into the chaotic wonder of adulthood. It holds the lessons I've gathered about love, life, and self-discovery. It's a reflection of who I am today, where I come from, and everything that has shaped me along the way.

I hope you enjoy the pages that follow. More than anything, I hope you find a piece of your own story in them.

This book is for anyone who's ever felt lost, hopeless, or out of place. I'm here to tell you—you will find your way. And you'll be just fine.

Acknowledgements

Here, there and everywhere

I was born with a big head,
 Quite literally,
 And figuratively, a head
 Full of tangled thoughts
 And entire worlds too large
 For this short existence to hold.

I was born feeling out of place,
 In a world that wanted
 Me to *find* my place,
 Leaving me fragmented,
 Even as I tried, over and over,
 To fit in, if only for a moment.

My thoughts were butterflies --
 Fleeting, floating, never really landing.
My emotions were storms --
 Too intense and raw to be contained.
My attention was a kaleidoscope --
 Constantly shifting colors and shapes.

I was caged one day, flying the next --
 A pendulum swinging between chaos and calm,
 A radio switching stations every other second.

They called it scattered,
 I called it *everywhere all at once,*
A mind stretched across multiple universes,
 Processing problems no one noticed.

They asked me to slow down,
 But how do you slow the wind?
They told me I should fit in,
 But I wasn't made for boxes.
They said I need to socialize,
 When I was the lonely one.

I was the daydreamer in class,
 Staring out the windows, writing stories,
While the teacher droned on about fractions
 Even as I solved them in the fraction of a second.

I was the smart kid
 Who talked too much,
The one always *almost* getting there,
 But never quite.

I was too serious for my own good,
 Too in my head, too silent,
Yet I was building castles inside,
 With a joy too pure for the world around.

I never fit their mold,
 But now I know, I was never meant to.
I was not broken,
 I was just built different.
I was brilliance wrapped in chaos.
 I was lightning in a bottle.

I may not always be here,
 I was meant to be everywhere,
 Amidst pages half-filled,
 Writing tales yet to be told.

And I will make it,
 Even if I take the long way there --
 Here, there, and everywhere.

Thalial

Thalial, otherwise known as,
Thazhuviya Mahadevar Kovil Street --
A little alley in the heart of Nagercoil,
A town lost in time
In the seas of Kanyakumari,
Etched in the southern corner of India,
A town as timeless as when the seas
Formed around it.

A beach town.
A quiet tourist spot.
A bustling trading center.
A beautiful amalgamation of communities,
And of three oceans.
But to me, it always meant --
Home.
Hometown.
Laughter, coming from somewhere deep inside my soul.

To me, it always meant --
Tiny long houses
Filled with big hearted people,
The houses lined up with vast verandahs
And wide open indoor *muthams*

Which would fill up with water
During the rainy season, as us kids
Splashed about in glee.

To me, it always meant --
The beginning of a new day as the *diyas*
Went up in the big temple at the
End of the street,
Even as a devotional song played from
The speakers, signifying the dawn has come.

To me, it always meant --
The '*sundal*' cart that came in the evenings,
With a ring of a bell all too familiar,
Even after all these years.
And my favorite road-side eatery
My dad would buy from twice a week,
That '*chapathi and kuruma*' dish,
The taste of which will always remain
Behind in my tongue, till the day I die.

To me, it always meant --
The chaos of Pongal,
When the whole street comes alive,
Kolams with white, red, pink, colored powders
In front of all the houses,
Everyone, old and young,

Is out and about, taking part as an entire
Community comes together,
To dance and sing and celebrate
The land and all its abundance.

To me, it always meant --
The sands and the salty air of Kanyakumari,
The bustling traffic at Kottar,
The madness of the market at Vadasery,
The sprawling complexes at Manimedai,
The magnificent splendour of the Thiruparappu falls,
To me, this was the world.

Thalial, otherwise known as,
Thazhuviya Mahadevar Kovil Street --
From one corner with the divine, stone temple
To the other with a Peepul tree older than generations,
This little street is the place I was born into.
This is where I grew up,
And no matter where I go,
I shall always find my way back home to Thalial.

Father's daughter

To the world, my father
Is a lively man,
The one with the loudest voice in the room,
A friend anyone can lean on,
A supportive husband,
A doting dad,
A responsible sibling,
A caring son.

But here I am, to show you,
The untold pages of his story.

My father was born
Into a world which was never really his own.
Losing his mother at two,
His father at five,
His parents were mere memories he once had.
Passed into the safe hands of his uncle,
His roots turned borrowed.

He was the youngest of five,
Yet wise beyond years,
His childhood slipped away even before he knew.
His dreams soared to

Heights that the people surrounding him
Could never even comprehend,
Yet the weight of those around held him
Down, even as he reached for the sun.

Still, he persevered, through
The stormy seas, ever looking for the
Silver lining
In a dark cloud,
He never gave up on hope.
Success, he decided,
Was in his own hands,
And built a life of quiet dignity,
Brick by humble brick.

He never knew
The soft warmth of a mother's lap,
Nor the firm assurance of a father's hand—
Yet, to me,
He gave the world.

Everyone says I was born to look like
My father, but I know now --
I was born to *live* like him.

In my voice,
In my tangled web of thoughts,

In my unquenchable thirst for success,
In my dreams and my fears,
I carry pieces of him,
I carry with me his unfulfilled dreams.

From talking incessantly,
To always seeing the silver lining,
From walking unevenly,
To always striving for perfection,
From impulses to insecurities,
From falling down to rising back up,
I see my father in everything
I do,
I am *him*.

I am my father's daughter,
Made by his genes,
Shaped by his resilience,
Built by his sacrifices.
And one day,
I will fulfill the dreams he never could,
And show the world
That I am the daughter
Of a man who refused to break,
That, I am, in fact, my father's daughter.

First steps

The first time I walked
Onto a stage,
A little girl in navy blue uniform
And pigtails tied up with a red ribbon,
Clutching a crumpled white paper
Layered with sweat from my shaking hands.

Every step up the mahogany stairs
To the podium,
Looming like a mountain of doom
Stuck in a sea of lava,
Felt like my very last.

I wished the wooden floor would give way
Into the very center of the Earth,
So I could disappear and
Never come back.

I placed my iron-like feet
Which refused to move,
On the short step meant to give me elevation,
Just enough to reach the microphone,
Even as my throat closed up
Threatening never to open again.

Sweat beads gathered on my face,
and in places
I never knew existed.

My stomach churned,
Dangerously similar to that time
I fell sick in a car driving up a mountain.

My hands and legs quivered, my eyes
Moistened with little tears, and my ears
Rang with the echoes of my peers:
Students chattering in excitement,
Teachers in the back discussing who might win,
Pens clicking in judges' hands,
Weapons, ready for the kill.

Then,
the soft tiny *ding* of the timer.

Almost too soft to hear,
yet piercing enough
To send a jolt of horror
Through the bravest of hearts.

The many practice sessions with Ma flashed in my head
Like a movie montage

Replayed as the main character dies.
Except,
I was very much alive.

For a moment, I froze.
Then, 'A very good morning!' rolled out of my mouth
Even before I knew.

Three minutes.

I spoke, I lived, I transformed,
Into another world, for a whole
Three minutes.

Three minutes,
Which felt like three hours,
For what I'd prepared for three weeks.

And three hours later,
I was not number three.
Not number ten, either.
I was *one*.

The first time I walked onto a stage,
I won the first place.
And there was no looking back.

Period, period.

A drop,
A strange red,
Such was the beginning of my womanhood.

On a glorious day,
The sun was smiling wide,
And so was I, until
I woke up with blood,
Without war, without injury,
Nothing had changed, yet everything had changed.
Glancing at the red drops,
Life flashing before my eyes,
I decided I was done.

Menstruation, they said,
Puberty, they said,
But all I saw was red.
I had blossomed into a flower,
So they said,
I had got my first period.
Well, period,
I said to it,
You made me miss my first period!

A love ballad

Let me tell you a tale of love,
Where eyes meet and hearts merge,
When the divine threads of fate intertwine,
For such was the tale of Music and Dance.

He had always listened, only listened.
Afraid he might lose himself in his own beauty.
Such was his life, until she came.

A gentle soul, dancing her way onto this mortal Earth.
She was a sight to behold.
And my, how blind had he been!

Universe had played a cruel joke:
He saw now, while she listened,
The song of his soul glowing in front of him.

He should have known, she was too good to be his.
So she said.
And arrogance killed his arrogance.

He retreated into himself, sadness was born.
The world trembled at this new aura he carried.
A melody full of sorrow echoed from him.

He drowned one day, too broken by love.

She wept, knowing she had done something terrible.
Her heart ached for him,
Lamenting now, that it was too late.

Too late, he said,
As he watched her from Heaven,
A ghost descending upon the Earth.

Wait for me, she whispered.
Shackles, she said, are my life.
She could not escape them.

I will wait for you, he said,
Across a thousand lifetimes.
Yet, she was never to be his.

He was a free spirit,
She, a slave to her creators.
They never could be together.
Not while the Earth still breathed.

And so they live on, to this day,
Dance, tapping away her time,
As Music muses silently above,
Both waiting for eternity to end.

Such is the tale of Music and Dance,
Separated by life,
Bound by fate,
They wait, for that fraction of a second,
When he is summoned by humans,
And she dances in glee at his arrival,
Extending her hands for his embrace,
And in that moment, they are one.

Letter to Ma

Somewhere between growing up in a large household
Where everyone was expected to do their share of the
chores,
To working hard to be independent
And earn some money for your struggling parents,
You forgot to be a child, Ma.

Somewhere between getting married young
Into a large, multi-generational family
Which was more hierarchical than a government office,
And supporting Pa through job losses and financial
crises,
You forgot to be a child, Ma.

Somewhere between taking care of me,
Sitting down with me to do my homework in 1st grade
To calming me down through a panic attack in 12th
grade,
You forgot to be a child, Ma.

Somewhere between taking care of your ageing parents,
To supporting me through corporate life,
When will you ever be a child, Ma?

When will you be free, of chores, and explore the world
With an innocent child-like wonder?
When will you be taken care of, instead of taking care of
others?
When will you ever be a child, Ma?

Somewhere between now and the future,
I hope I can give you back your childhood, Ma,
To be the little young Vani who dreamt of adventures,
Of being a lawyer,
And writing poetry and stories,
Who hoped to see the cherry blossoms of Japan
And the winding waters of Venice,
Who for once, wanted to be taken care of, instead
Of being the one giving care,
Who laughed from the bottom of her heart,
Without a single worry in the world.
Somewhere between now and the future,
I hope that one day,
Even if for a little moment,
I can give you back your childhood, Ma.

Burned by the sun

There once was a girl named Kat,
She was brilliant,
She was vivacious,
She could learn anything she wanted to,
Yet, the one thing she could never learn,
Was to unlearn.

Dream big, her father said. She
learned to reach for the stars.
Then he came again, and said,
It is now time to stop,
Lest she was burned by the sun.
But she didn't know how to stop.

Work hard, her mother said. She
Toiled day and night, with a thirst
That never died. Her mother
Came back, and said,
It is now time to stop.
But she was too far gone to stop.

Be humble, her teacher said. So
She spent years shrinking
Herself, only to later be

Told she should speak louder
Than others, but it was too
Late for her to simply stop.

They said -- Be strong. Be perfect. Be disciplined.
Be graceful. Be silent. Be patient.
Be a good girl. Be a proper woman.
Yet no one ever taught her --
Be weak. Be sensitive. Be confident. No one said
To not be okay, to not have it together all the time,
To live not for others but for herself,
To fail, to fall, to stop.
She kept going, through sunshine and shadow.
And one day, she burst into flames,
Just like her father once said.
She really did fly too close to the sun.

Is this love?

Baby, pull me close,
Let me drown in your breath.
Put your arms around me,
Let us dance,
Dance, dance and just dance,
Like there is no tomorrow.

Take my hands
And feel the music flowing through my skin,
Feel the electricity.
It's just us,
You and me all night,
Fused into one.

Oh, is this what love feels like?
Stuck in a haze,
Oh baby,
Let's freeze time.
The wind on my face,
I'm soaring, come lift me up.

I'm lost,
In your sea of curls,
Let us meet,

Our eyes,
Our smiles,
Our lips.

Look at me, baby,
Read my eyes instead.
Break this eerie silence,
And come find me.
I sneak a look at you
The world around me is blur.

Ragged breaths,
Racing thoughts,
All I can see is you.
Look at me,
Let us make chaos together,
Oh, is this love?

Baby, this is
Heavens come down
Upon this Earth,
This is being
Awake, after all this time.
This is alive.

To my Primrose

206,
Just a number, right?
To us, it's an emotion,
The beginning of our epic journey,
And the rest, as they say,
History.

The back bench shenanigans
In our first semester,
The thousand tea breaks
We took in the last,
Oh, how far we have come.

Through the highs and lows,
Through laughter and tears,
Through your songs and my TV shows,
Through my worst and yours,
Through college and beyond,
Here we are, our bond intact.

To the uninitiated,
We argue a lot.
But only we know,
It is love in disguise.

You act, I think.
Extrovert versus introvert.
I over plan, you run with the flow,
We may be
Divided by our differences, but
United by love.

Remember the times we walked to class together,
After I waited for you as you were always late.
Remember when Vicky and I would annoy you
With our 'how to get away with murder' talk.
Remember the time we attended reverse coding
And I was no help.
All the extra labs,
The chais and gossips we shared,
A thousand conversations under the Wi-Fi tree,
And the plans we made,
Just a tiny fragment
Of the million little moments we had.

From making fun
Of your constant singing,
To being in awe with the crowd,
Swaying to your Senthoora,
You and I have grown together,
The Primrose to my Katniss.

From our personality types
To our zodiac signs
We were a perfect fit.
I know now,
We were meant to be.

Time has gone and passed,
I'm still back on day one,
When I met the girl with
The big eyes staring at me
And the big earrings glaring at me.

You were there on that first day,
And I will be there with you, my KC,
My best friend of this lifetime,
Till the last one.

Lost in transit

One day
I'll look in the mirror
And I'll see my own self
Instead of a thousand fragments.
My battle scars shall stop bleeding
And shine with the tales of my stormy past,
My laughter will echo across the air, my eyes
Will twinkle again with golden light, just like the
Happy little girl in the picture framed in my home,
Lost in a dream far away, spinning new stories, the
World her oyster, and an innocent smile on her face.
That day, I'll look in the mirror and see my true self,
Raw with all my emotions unmasked and my
Inner child undeterred by the weight of a
Neurotypical world. My thoughts shall
Finally stay afloat, without me drifting
Into dark, silent corners. One day I'll
Look into the mirror, and see only
Me. Not you, not the version
You want of me, just me,
Finally, me.

Someday, somewhere

Maybe we will meet again, someday,
Within the flash of a silver lightning,
On a stormy monsoon evening,
As the sunshine yellow sky melts into
A tangerine orange dusk,
Just like that first time.

Maybe we have already met
Across several golden threads of fate,
Our eyes always seeking the other
In the midst of all others,
Always finding each other,
Like a compass set towards home.

Maybe it was a coincidence, or
A cosmic connection.
We were like moths drunk on light,
Drawn to the flame, yet in the end
Burned to ashes,
By a flame called love.

Maybe we were never meant to be,
It was just an illusion,
A fever dream in pastel hues,

Only real in our heads.
It was a flickering rainbow,
A wish upon a star.

Maybe I'll wake up one day and
Be in your soft arms again.
Maybe we'll meet again, someday,
Somewhere, a lifetime or two later,
And the world around us will fade into
A blank canvas, just as it began.

The storm before the calm

It is not the heights of success,
Not the glorious days that make you.
It is the dark moments,
Silent and sudden,
In the middle of the night,
When there is no one,
Not one person or thing to distract you.
It is those dark moments,
When your demons come out to play,
And you're not whole,
That define you.
Your success can only get to your head,
But the darkness,
It grows on you
Until it fuses with your very being.
So tonight is for the one
Whose battle with darkness
Rages on as the night falls,
Know this:
You may not be at your best, but
You're fighting on,
Even at your worst,
And that makes you the best
You can ever be.

Even when all else seems lost,
And the storm looms large,
Know this:
This too shall pass.
The calm will come for you,
And all will be well again.
A new day will come,
A better day will come,
And the storm will give way
To the calm.

Today, I am reborn

I see death
Of the feelings I parted with years ago,
Of my fears
That held me back,
Because the only fear is fear itself,
Of my old self,
She didn't serve me well anyway.

As I stand on the edge
Of the snow-capped peaks
Spread out across me,
My toes hurt,
But my heart doesn't, anymore.

I look at the valley of Spiti
And it speaks to me, like an ancient sage,
Of letting go,
Of my fears,
Of my broken tears,
Of the weight of a life
Which had become too much to bear.

Amidst the bone-chilling winds,
The endless jagged mountains,

And the glaring, looming snow,
In this winter wonderland,
At last, I have found myself again.

I see death
Of the pain which had surrounded
My soul, of the uncertainty
Which had come to be the norm,
Of the insecurities
Etched deep inside,
By a world which was never really right.

This was the end of my life
As I knew it, the one
Which was never really for me.
In this middle land,
I am reborn,
Fresh as snow on a cold winter day,
Flowing freely as the river,
Standing tall like the Himalayas,
And ready to just be
As I am, as
All that I am.
Today, under the clearest sky
I have ever seen,
Under a million twinkling stars,
I am reborn.

Homecoming

The long halls,
Of the hundred-year-old house, in
The narrow streets of **Nagercoil**,
Where everyone knew everyone,
And everything was out in the open,
A childhood in slow motion,
Such was the home I grew up in.

Underneath the neem tree,
Outside the window in my parents' house,
With sunsets and heartfelt conversations,
I learned to spread my wings,
At my home in **Chennai**,
A city in transition,
Just like me.

Living on my own means,
Within the beige walls of my flat,
Steering life on my own terms,
In cosmopolitan **Bengaluru**,
I have lost and found myself,
Amidst the fresh blossoms and disco nights,
In this first home away from home.

In the quiet mornings of
Pune, with chai in hand and
A city filled with chaotic auto rides, and traffic
Which never dies, I learned
To find home in new places and
New people, and find comfort
In the idea of never really having one place to call home.

Home,
What does it mean?
Which one does it mean?
Is it one of the many places
That have made me,
Or the wide blue sky
That calls to me,
Or in the work that I do,
The people that I love?
Maybe home is the whole universe,
Maybe home is a person,
Maybe home is nothing but an illusion.

Now,
I have learned to find my home,
Wherever life takes me,
In the nostalgic lanes of Nagercoil,
In the evening breeze at my parents' place,
Amidst the ancient pillars of my ancestral house,

From the silence of my Bengaluru apartment,
To the chaos of Pune,
From the rocks of Kanyakumari,
To the sands of Marina.
Wherever my journey takes me,
I find a little bit of home,
In the people that I meet,
In the places that I live in,
In the very air of the cities I visit,
In the end, home is
Within me, and always within me,
Wherever I shall go.

Beyond labels

<u>Labels</u> could never define what I feel.

You call it *anxiety*,
I call it a thousand neurons firing all at once,
As if my very being could shatter any moment.
It's that one song running in a broken loop,
Not a melody, but a chaotic rap battle with
Someone screaming the verses over and over.

You call it *depression*,
I call it a black hole I've been pushed into.
I can't breathe, I can't talk, I can't feel,
Because I don't exist in that world.
I just float round in endless silence
Like a ghost moving in eternal slow motion,
To be chipped at bit by bit until I'm gone.

You call it *burnout*,
I call it the weight of a world which doesn't pause
Even when I break.

You call it my *imagination*,
I call it my mind attacking my own mind,
A never-ending civil war.

You call it a *delusion*,
I call it alternate realities, the size of which
You cannot begin to comprehend.

You call it *overthinking*,
"Being inside your head too much",
A trivial problem to "just snap out of".
I call it dying a slow death on the inside,
An invisible ailment I wouldn't wish upon by worst
enemies,
A problem which is trivial until it's too dangerous.

You dismiss these labels,
You're right to, because...
<u>Labels</u> could never define what I feel.

The art, the artist

I often wonder what happens to poets
Who lose their words,
Having drifted far away into a place
Where the universe serves no inspiration anymore.

Can an artist even be called an artist
Without their art?

I often fear a day will come
When my own words run out,
Having drifted far away,
Or be forced to, by this journey called life.

Will I still be the person that I am
If not for the words which represent all that I am?

I often wonder what happens to art itself
As we go through the motions of living,
Does life stand in the way of making art,
Or does it make way for more art?

Maybe art is meant to feed into life,
Maybe life into art.

In a world where words aren't our own anymore
As man and machine become one,
And the world moves on to other things,
I wonder if I should be a poet at all.

In the end, I shall choose this suffering
Over and over, because without art,
There is no artist. Without my words,
There is no me.

The circle of life

You tell me to live to my best,
I ask what do I live for?
Which side of me do I live for?
Do I fly free like a bird,
Letting the wind take its course?
Or do I stay still like a statue,
Never really moving, but
Always standing tall?

Life is a battle,
Fighting for your dreams,
While still paying the bills.
Holding on to my inner child,
While bearing the weight of adulthood.

Life is the world telling you
To be the best version of yourself,
While also whispering,
Slow down before you burn.

We're all naught but half-broken,
Drowning out our sorrows,
Even as we begin each day anew,
With fresh hope and smiles on our faces.

Maybe we were meant to be
Running forever, stuck in a loop like Sisyphus,
Moving forward and backward,
Dreaming of a mountaintop
That never really existed.

Maybe someday
It will all fall into place,
Maybe it never really will.

In the end, life is not a battle,
But a mountain to surrender to.
The struggle shall remain:
To find a balance
Between the bird and the statue.
I struggle to find it today,
So did those who came before me,
So will those who come after.
Such is the circle of life.

What healing looks like

This is what healing looks like.
The light at the end of a long tunnel.
A single ray of hope.
Turbulence. Serenity.
Ugly tears and a runny nose.
The calm before the storm.
The eye of the storm.
Slaying old demons,
Fighting new ones.
Digging deeper and deeper,
With no end in sight.
Accountability,
For yourself, and others.
The joy of little wins, the pain of setbacks.
Trauma, and the slow aftermath.
Letting go, letting back in.
To forgive and be forgiven.
Anger, sadness and joy,
A burst of emotions, then none.
Uncertainty, and, out of nowhere, clarity.
Acceptance. Resilience.
A moment of calm,
Before another storm.
This is what healing looks like.

Forever begins now

It was always going to be you; I know that now.

Love like this comes
Once in several lifetimes, yet our eyes met amidst a
Vast ocean of people drifting through this momentary
Existence called life. Is this what they call destiny?

You came into my life
On a beautiful spring day, dropped in by some
Unseen force -- our threads intertwined forever.

And in your eyes, I found myself again. Litte did I
Know, you were the
Saviour who would
Hold my hands as I reached for the light
Again. You're not just a part of me,
You are the best part.

My love for you is not always
Out loud, but it is
Raw, radiant, relentless.
Even forever doesn't feel enough to hold it in.

They say we met just a few moments ago --
How do I explain I've known you now
Across lifetimes? I
Never want to not have known you.

Any time I write about love, it's your
Name which appears before me now.
You, my love, are my favorite reason for everything.
The world may change around me, but you
Hold me steady on this earth.
In you, I've found my everything.
Nothing else matters now that you're here.
Given another chance, I would only find you sooner.

If I lived before our paths crossed, then it wasn't
Nearly a life at all.

Through the storms and the rainbows,
Holding on to you has been the easiest thing.
Every day with you feels like the start of another story.

Whether it's now or 50 years later, I shall choose you --
Over and over, through
Rain and sunshine. Life will always be right,
Long as you're by my side,
Day after day, in loops and spirals -- now and forever.

The girl who was too much

"You study too much", said a friend
    Who was not so much a friend
When I was all of ten.

"You talk too much",
    My favourite teacher advised,
I had just turned twelve.

"You think too much", said the crush,
    My first real one, that made your heart flutter,
At fifteen.

"You dream too much", scolded,
    Mom and Dad, as I turned twenty,
And walked away from childhood.

"You read too much"
    "You plan too much"
"You care too much"
    "You feel too much"

I was, the world had branded, too much.
    Too much, too little, but,
Never enough.

Too loud. Too awkward. Too serious. Too cold.
　　Too emotional. Too dreamy. Too structured.

Too loud those for those who cannot match my energy.
　　Too awkward for those who only want reflections
of themselves.
Too serious for those who refuse the joy in me.
　　Too cold yet too emotional for those whose
emotions are different than mine.
Too dreamy for those who dare not reach for the stars.
　　Too structured for the unstructured.

I was, the world had branded, too much.
　　Too much. Too little.
Never enough.

Now I know, I was never meant,
　　To be *just* enough.

I was a flaming phoenix
　　Living in a world of gliding swans.

I am, and will always be,
　　Too much.

www.ingramcontent.com/pod-product-compliance
Lightning Source LLC
LaVergne TN
LVHW010020200726
843495LV00015B/1853